JOURNEY INTO LIFE

Journey into life

INHERITING THE STORY OF EARLY FRIENDS

Gerald Hewitson

THE 2013 SWARTHMORE LECTURE

First published May 2013

Quaker Books, Friends House, 173 Euston Road, London NW1 2BJ

www.quaker.org.uk

978-1-907123-47-4

Book designed and typeset by: Cox Design, Witney

Printed by: RAP Spiderweb, Oldham

FSC
www.fsc.org
MIX
Paper from
responsible sources
FSC® C011842

THE SWARTHMORE LECTURE

The Swarthmore lectureship was established by the Woodbrooke Extension Committee at a meeting held 9 December 1907: the minute of the committee providing for an "annual lecture on some subject relating to the message and work of the Society of Friends".

The name Swarthmore was chosen in memory of the home of Margaret Fox, which was always open to the earnest seeker after Truth, and from which loving words of sympathy and substantial material help were sent to fellow workers.

The lectureship continues to be under the care of Woodbrooke Quaker Study Centre Trustees, and is a significant part of the education work undertaken at and from Woodbrooke. The lectureship has a twofold purpose: first, to interpret to the members of the Society of Friends their message and mission; and second, to bring before the public the spirit, aims and fundamental principles of Friends. The lecturers alone are responsible for any opinions expressed.

The lectureship provides both for the publication of a book and for the delivery of a lecture, the latter usually at the time of Britain Yearly Meeting of the Society of Friends. A lecture related to the present book was delivered at Yearly Meeting in London on the evening of Saturday 25 May 2013.

The Swarthmore Lecture Committee can be contacted via the Clerk, c/o Woodbrooke Quaker Study Centre, 1046 Bristol Road, Selly Oak, Birmingham B29 6LJ.

CONTENTS

ACKNOWLEDGEMENTS

I should like to dedicate this text to the memory of my father.

Even such a slim document as this owes a great deal to others. I am very grateful to the Swarthmore Lecture Committee for their invitation to offer the lecture. It proved a way of bringing into focus much of what had been happening in my life. In the event the writing proved to be a mini journey in its own right – for me and, I suspect, for them. Beth Allen and Jan Arriens were unstintingly supportive.

The generous heart of Joanne Klassen and the reach of her Life Writing for Transformation project never ceases to amaze me. I am grateful for her continuing friendship.

The Friends I encountered at Quaker Life, both staff and committee members, contributed far more than they will ever know.

Woodbrooke staff have been consistently generous with their patience and considerable expertise, ever willing to engage in the next conversation, facilitate the next insight.

In 2011, during the Fall Term, Gwyneth and I were Resident Friends at Pendle Hill. I shall remain ever grateful for the opportunity to visit this remarkable place, and meet the Friends we encountered there. Doug Gwyn's conversations were particularly missed when we left. He, along with Ben Pink Dandelion, John Punshon, Penelope Cummins and Alan Johnson, provided kind and helpful comments at various stages.

I have been very fortunate indeed in the strength, vitality and depth of my local meeting in Holyhead. They have helped me to find the power in the words of *Advices and queries* 18:

> Seek to know one another in the things which are eternal, bear the burden of each other's failings and pray for one another. As we enter with tender sympathy into the joys and sorrows of each other's lives, ready to give help and to receive it, our meeting can be a channel for God's love and forgiveness.

Wyn Rowlands and Fiona Owen, in particular, will recognise the path described here. We have walked an Emmaus path together.

My friend Steve Parker has been a faithful companion, constantly offering encouragement and appreciation. Shelagh Robinson guided me through the Equipping for Ministry course at Woodbrooke, and many of the experiences which are the basis for this pamphlet. Linda Murgatroyd, with her gentle voice, was a consistently insightful reader. Iris Webster was one of a number of Friends who spent time in prayer on behalf of me and this project.

In Friends House, Louisa Wright was a responsive editor, and Peter Daniels a thoughtful copy-editor, ensuring clarity where things were muddy, and careful, thorough checking of references.

John and Diana Lampen know the extent of their joint contribution to this text. As for my family, Gwyneth, Siân, Angharad, Rhodri and Aled, between them they teach me the costs and considerable joys of discipleship.

Despite all this help and support, I am painfully aware of the inadequacies of the lecture. I alone remain responsible for these.

Introduction

As Quakers, stories are important to us: the stories of our religious society, of individual Quakers in the past, of our meetings and our religious life together and the stories we tell with our own lives. These stories inspire us, challenge us, humble us and guide us. They both hint at the truth beyond words, and allow the listener to take from them the truth they are ready to receive at that time. In our Quaker tradition, which rests on experience rather than abstractions, our stories are a way of making manifest our experience. Just as written Testimonies to the Grace of God in the lives of dead Friends hold up the story of a life and reflect the spirit shown in that life, so the stories of contemporary Friends become living testimonies.

This year's Swarthmore Lecture is one Friend's story. It is a story of convincement and of transformation; it has resonances with the stories told by Friends throughout their history, and speaks of an experience which is available to us all.

Just as with any story there will be words, metaphors and concepts used which we might find new, difficult or uncomfortable as well as ones which will be familiar and accessible. As with all stories we need to look for the spirit and the message behind the words, for that is where the power lies.

The text in this book is the basis of the spoken lecture given by Gerald in May 2013. The Swarthmore Lecture Committee invited Gerald to give a spoken lecture because of his gifts in teaching and spoken ministry and because of the personal story he has to tell. This publication supports those gifts, making them available to those Friends who were unable to be present at the spoken ministry and to enable those who were there to revisit and reflect on it. An audio recording of the spoken lecture will also be available afterwards on the Woodbrooke website www.woodbrooke.org.uk or on compact disc from Woodbrooke. You will find suggested activities for reflection and study by individuals and groups on pages 47–53.

Helen Rowlands
Head of Education, Woodbrooke Quaker Study Centre

Journey into Life

The words on the meeting house were a genuine invitation:

> Quakers are people of different beliefs, lifestyles and social backgrounds. What we have in common is an acceptance that all people are on a spiritual journey. We hope that we are indeed a real society of Friends, open to the world and welcoming everyone.

Initially, some thirty years earlier, it was this sense of the openness of the spiritual journey that helped me into membership. And yet now I found these words bland, anodyne – in attempting to exclude none, to be inoffensive, to convey no hint of dangerous fervour or undesirable conviction, they said little that was not trite or commonplace. Was this what we contemporary Quakers had created? A belief-free zone into which anyone could step without any sense of conviction? A group of well-meaning friends who spoke of friendship, but not of commitment? Who offered a spiritual journey without indicating the inevitable concomitant of sacrifice? What had changed in me that I should find these words so difficult now – words which I would have found attractive all those years ago because of their very openness?

As many of us do, I had discovered Quakers as an adult. Unlike many today, who come into membership in later life, I entered into membership in my early thirties. So for most of my adult life I have been a Quaker. For most of my life I have lived by secular values.

Quakers are non-credal, and this to me meant that I was free of any obligation to any beliefs. Indeed, the feature I valued was being able to range widely in my thinking. Some of my earliest Quaker mentors in Cambridge were capable of drawing widely on spiritual language from a number of religions. I had no experience of God. God was a concept I tried, from time to time, to understand. I lived my life by well-meaning liberal values, albeit ones which were informed by the decencies of Quakerism. My root motivations were laid down in a difficult childhood and played out in an utterly demanding work environment.

But there have been important changes in my life. I now live, albeit imperfectly and falteringly, in a world of apocalyptic revelation of God's love streaming through the universe for each and every one of us. I do not fear the word apocalypse. Its original meaning is one of uncovering, or revealing. In this sense, early Friends, as well as Jesus, lived in a world of apocalyptic revelation – they lived in a world which had been revealed to them, a world where they saw that infinite love was the first motion. They trusted this perception, with a deep and abiding faith; indeed, the origin of the word faith is to trust. So great was their faith, their trust in the world revealed to them, that they lived out the consequences despite all difficulty. On the basis of this life-affirming trust, they were willing to die.

Living in a liberal democracy as I do, I very much doubt that my faith, my trust, will ever need to be tested in quite the same way. Nevertheless, I attempt to live with the difficulties and joys of a life being guided and directed. My life is not my own. I recognise I was shaped for a purpose, the meaning of which is entirely beyond me, and my role is to undertake, however falteringly and unsteadily, the necessary activities in order to listen carefully to my next step in an unfolding path, which not only offers guidance, but draws me into a new sense of community.

What brought about such a profound reorientation of my life? It occurred late in life, over a number of years, and had different aspects. The starting point was to hear, truly hear, the words of George Fox:

Now I was come up in spirit through the flaming sword into

the paradise of God. All things were new, and all the creation gave another smell unto me than before, beyond what words can utter.[1]

Initially my sense was of a great unburdening. Then these words acted as a spark to a flame. In seeking to understand what they meant in the lives of other early Friends and the origins of Quakers, it seemed as if I was following a thread in a labyrinth. As I penetrated deeper and deeper, more seemed to be revealed – a book, a conversation, an insight, a revelation – and Way opened.[2]

I am not a scholar. My mind is too slow for the deliberate accumulation of data and details which help an original insight to appear. So I am immensely grateful to those scholars who opened up the world of early Quakers for me.

I saw early Quakers as offering insight into my state of mind and where I was in my life – that which Quakers call 'my condition'. All the great religions are simply attempts to explain back to us this complex, messy, difficult business of being alive. This business in which we trip up, fall, make mistakes, err; the process of living in which we are hurt, sometimes dreadfully hurt; where we hurt others, sometimes equally dreadfully, and often we hurt this beautiful planet which is our world. Early Friends are no different in this regard. They describe for us our capacity to be human. So if we can hear them, their words offer a strength and a vigour, a depth and clarity of spiritual awareness and understanding which can offer us insights into our own condition, and thereby into the human condition. And it is by seeing their world as fully as we can that we can begin to hear what they say to us today.

The early Friends

One of the striking things about early Friends is that they speak and act from a place of complete conviction. This deep conviction was a result of their experience. In the deep silence of their gathered meetings, they had 'seen' a new world order. Then, as today, the world was constructed on the human values of awarding privilege and status to wealth and power. Some current religious groups describe this as

Babylon, or 'the domination system' – a world ruled by the power of wealth, influence, and ultimately naked aggression, locked into conspicuous consumption while others starve. Those who consider themselves to be pragmatists, or who believe themselves to possess a down to earth view of how things work will often call this the 'real' world. It is a world whose strength is so apparently overwhelming that it seems it must last eternally – as the Roman Empire must have once seemed to those who lived under its dominion, as Jesus and his early followers did. Early Friends saw these values of this 'real world' were not only false in themselves, but that they were inimical to the Presence with whom they were intimate, and who required a world based on equality, peace, justice and mercy. Many people saw the world as it is, and could see no further; Quakers saw the world as God wishes it to be – not a world based on might and strength, but on a long-suffering loving-kindness, imitating the cosmic patience which unceasingly offers its love to the world, wishes us no harm, is solicitous of our welfare, and wants nothing but infinite good.

Edward Burrough:
We are not for names, nor men, nor titles of government,
nor are we for this party or against the other… but we are for
justice and mercy and truth and peace and true freedom, that
these may be exalted in our nation.[3]

Through these eyes, they came to see that the world exerts a stranglehold on perception, and that most people live in accordance with its flawed ideas and dislocated values. Quakers, while being fully alive and alert to the everyday, moved and had their being in a different space, living out their new perception, modelling a new way of being which was in this world, but not of this world.

Entry into this new world order, this place they stood in and knew intimately, was through their experience of encounter. All religions strive to describe the experience of human beings meeting a final, absolute reality. It is in this encounter that human beings find meaning and purpose. Unless we are extremely unfortunate in our journey through the Society of Friends we all know when we have experienced a gathered meeting: a meeting where the silence is as soft as velvet, as deep as a still pool; a silence where words emerge, only to deepen and enrich that rich silence, and where Presence is as palpable and soft as the skin of a peach; where the membrane separating this moment in time and eternity is filament-fine. It is in these circumstances that we can trust our experience, know that we are in the presence of "a creative Energy that has birthed us and totally accepts us, unfolding an abundance of life for us, desiring we should be made whole. The Power is as intimate to us as breath and blood; it is intrinsically within us as we, and all things, are in its embrace."[4]

I had this experience quite regularly over a lengthy personal Quaker history, but had not learned to trust it. I had not made it the basis of my life. It was only when my life as I had constructed it was ending – my work ceasing, ambitions unfulfilled, children leaving home – that I found myself in "the dark night journey of the soul", a place Sandra Cronk describes so well as where "All the finite things we used to cling to are now revealed to be incapable of bearing the weight of the infinite."[5] In this condition, I saw the love of God streaming through the universe for each and every one of us – endlessly, ceaselessly, cascading as a benign flood. Early Quaker writings became not a source of academic interest, but a description which helped explain who I was, how I had come to be.

Their encounter, and the sense they made of it, was the crucial factor in early Friends' definition of themselves and who they were, both as individuals and as a gathered people. At times they found the experience having the power to rip them open, at other times it possessed a sweet, gentle astringency. Then, as we do now, they struggled to find the right words to describe what had happened to them. They found they needed a range of metaphors to describe their experience beyond the ordinary and everyday, to describe this power at the heart of the encounter. So they used words like 'Inner Teacher', 'Light', 'Seed', 'Life', 'Anchor'.

George Fox:
My secret belief was stayed firm, and hope underneath held
me, as an anchor in the bottom of the sea... causing it to
swim above the sea where all the raging waves, foul weather,
tempests and temptations are.

I saw the harvest white and the Seed of God lying thick in the
ground, as ever did wheat that was sown outwardly, and none
to gather it.[6]

See also the works of Isaac Penington for these metaphors.[7]

Whichever metaphor they used, in whatever context, they found it to be a healing power, offering life lived at a deeper, richer level than that which they had previously experienced. This was a deeply Christian age; it was inevitable that Friends would turn to the language of the Bible to describe their sense of being new born into a different world. However, it was not just that the Bible provided a language for the experience. The Bible is, at heart, the continuing story of encounter, so it provided the patterns and examples whereby their new found, newly discovered experience was described and understood.

George Fox:
I saw that none could read John's words aright and with a true
understanding of them, [unless] in and with the same divine
Spirit by which John spoke them, and by his burning, shining
light, which is sent from God.[8]

Their Biblical reading did not dictate the terms of the encounter, but helped them capture the sense and meaning of their experience.

With their talk of Light, Seed and an Inner Teacher, Quakers strained the traditional language of Christianity as understood at the time. But unlike many of their religious contemporaries, they were not trying to teach the orthodoxy which had gathered about the life of Jesus; rather they were trying to describe the world they had discovered, which Jesus points to in his teaching, and his muddled followers tried to live out after his death. Quakers were Christians not in that they subscribed to the complex set of beliefs offered by the churches, but that they could confidently match their experiences with those that they read about in the Bible. They were a people of the book to the extent that they were not ruled by the letter of the law, but the power and authenticity of their encounter.

George Fox:
We had a meeting of many thousands of people a-top of a hill... and [Francis Howgill] saw they had no need of words for they were all sitting down under their teacher Christ Jesus; so he was moved to sit down again amongst them without speaking anything.[9]

Their fundamental experience was that individually and collectively they were an integral part of the divine order, not having to live a life in constant fear of falling short, or guilt that their life was not good enough. They did not live a life for which they had to atone, or for which anyone else had to atone on their behalf. Their present life was not a preparation for another life beyond death, in which all the contradictions, pains and difficulties of this life would be resolved: it was life on this earth which was full of promise and potential. As such, they could come to a state of blessedness, of inner holiness, in this material life, in this ordinary workaday world. It was the experience of quite ordinary people in extraordinary circumstances. It is an experience which is open to us, if we wish to enter into it.

As a group, Quakers recognised they possessed this sense of assured conviction that they had found and lived out a vital Truth – initially they called themselves the Friends of Truth. They described themselves as 'convinced'. But to be convinced was not, as in modern day parlance, to be intellectually persuaded of the rightness of an argument. Rather to be convinced was to be 'convicted of sin'. We need to be careful in reading this phrase. Generally speaking, as Quakers we do not like the word 'sin' – I do not like it myself, associated as it is with much poor teaching in churches from my early life. The way Quakers used this word sin is far more substantial and serious than the sometimes minor peccadilloes, often of a sexual nature, which are sometimes called sin. As early Quakers used the term, it described the sense that their whole lives as previously lived had proved empty, devoid of meaning and purpose. Even where they had lived a religious life, they had done this in accordance with the churches of the time, not in relation to the urgent, quickening Life which pulsed through them and the movement.

....

Isaac Penington:
"How may the principle of truth be discerned?" Answer: By
its piercing, quickening nature… for it appears and works, not
like man's reason or like motions of his mind which he takes
into the understanding part; but it appears and works livingly,
powerfully and effectually in the heart.[10]

....

On the basis of their experience, Quakers saw that the churches of the time taught the husk, not the vital life at the heart of religion. George Fox, when the Quakers were accused of "mumming and dumbing" in their worship, wrote:

Let the priest look to his own parish, how the people sit mumming and dumbing all their lifetime under him, that they may be always paying him; and why should we not sit under Christ, our Prophet, Shepherd, Bishop and Priest, and hear him?[11]

In this sense, their previous life had been lived by societal norms and human values. They had lived, as it were, in a place of shadow, when all along the blazing radiance of God's love had been available to them. So this word 'sinful' captured this sense of the hollowness of their previous existence; a life lived outside a relationship with the Seed, or Spirit.

This is part of the journey I had to make, from a modern liberalism to a full throated acceptance of the experiences and consequent insights of the seventeenth century. They strike me as having profound relevance today. It seems to me we need to hear that challenge, and undertake aspects of translation for ourselves. Because of the immediacy of my discoveries, I am learning to speak again. I find the language of seventeenth-century Quakers to be rich and redolent. My convincement is so recent and of such a kind that sometimes I am not able to translate seventeenth-century Quaker language into the modern day speech which might be preferred by some readers. I have barely learnt to speak it, let alone translate it.

The new life as experienced by early Friends, based on the immediacy and vibrancy of this meaningful encounter, they found to be full of promise, richness, affirmation and possibility. This new way of relating to all other people, and all of creation, they called the Kingdom of God. It is the world of peace and justice demanded by the prophets, and the world described by Jesus in his many parables and allusions.[12] It is built not by words and phrases, by observing ritual or custom or following the words of those the world has placed in authority. Instead, it was called into being by listening to the great energy they found in their meetings for worship, allowing this force to work with their inner power, thereby releasing strength into their lives, speaking through their deeds. This process is available to us today.

It was so clear, so real, so rich, full and meaningful, that Penington described it as Life. He showed in his writings that it is this Life which is to be sought:

I have met with my God... I have read his nature, his love, his compassions, his tenderness, which have melted, overcome and changed my heart before him.[13]

In pursuit of such boundless possibility, this sense of being fully alive, Penington advised a friend:

Give over thine own willing, give over thy own running, give over thine own desiring to know or be anything and sink down to the seed which God sows in the heart, and let that grow in thee and be in thee and breathe in thee and act in thee; and thou shalt find by sweet experience that the Lord knows that and loves and owns that, and will lead it to the inheritance of Life, which is its portion.[14]

That is, lay down personal desires to find accord with this larger life, this blessed purposefulness flowing through the universe. And anyone, regardless of background, wealth, status, education, could undertake this process of convincement, could place themselves 'in right ordering' with this power. In so doing, they also encountered this energy within themselves, in their own depths, for the power is both within and without. It is for this reason that some of the metaphors early Friends use speak of an internal reality, as well as an external – they speak of the 'Inner Teacher', and 'Christ within'. Thomas Kelly writes movingly of John Woolman's "presiding chairman" – a sort of 'inner clerk'– "It was as if there were in him a presiding chairman who, in the solemn, holy silence of inwardness, took the sense of the meeting".[15] Our inner clerk is, then, that voice which takes soundings of all our internal competing voices, and emerges with a firm measured clarity, offering a purposeful sense of direction.

Quakers found themselves being changed at the most intimate levels of their being, down to the level of their root motivation. From henceforth, from the time of their convincement, they were to be motivated not by arrogance or fear, guilt, anger or complacency, but by Truth. This Truth was not a series of propositions, but an inward condition of the heart. From this truth, a clear and convinced heart, Quakers could live a life of complete integrity. The word 'integrity' has at its root a word meaning 'wholeness' or 'blamelessness', and in this new state those early Friends felt themselves to be pure, holy, without sin. This might be as difficult for us to hear as it was for many people in those days. When I recognised what this meant for us as human beings and what it involved for me, my life was raised up. I believe it offers wonderful opportunities for our lives today. If we hear the words, it may have the same effect as it had on Margaret

Fell. When she heard George Fox in Ulverston Church, and his words penetrated her so that she felt as if the light was ripping her open, he was preaching the need for 'a circumcised heart'. It is a long quotation, but worth bearing with:

And when they were singing before the sermon, he came in; and when they had done singing, he stood up upon his seat or form and desired that he might have liberty to speak. And he that was in the pulpit said he might. And the first words that he spoke were as followeth: "He is not a Jew that is one outward, neither is that circumcision which is outward, but he is a Jew that is one inward, and that is circumcision which is of the heart". And so he went on and said, How that Christ was the Light of the world and lighteth every man that cometh into the world; and that by this Light they might be gathered to God, etc. And I stood up in my pew, and I wondered at his doctrine, for I had never heard such before. And then he went on, and opened the Scriptures, and said, "The Scriptures were the prophets' words and Christ's and the apostles' words, and what as they spoke they enjoyed and possessed and had it from the Lord". And said, "Then what had any to do with the Scriptures, but as they came to the Spirit that gave them forth. You will say, Christ saith this, and the apostles say this; but what canst thou say? Art thou a child of Light and hast walked in the Light, and what thou speakest is it inwardly from God?"

This opened me so that it cut me to the heart; and then I saw clearly we were all wrong. So I sat me down in my pew again, and cried bitterly. And I cried in my spirit to the Lord, "We are all thieves, we are all thieves, we have taken the Scriptures in words and know nothing of them in ourselves"... I saw it was the truth, and I could not deny it; and I did as the apostle saith, I "received the truth in the love of it". And it was opened to me so clear that I had never a tittle in my heart against it; but I desired the Lord that I might be kept in it, and then I desired no greater portion.[16]

If we look beyond the gender and cultural limitations which the term suggests (Fox was referring to Deuteronomy 30:6), this can indicate to us that Quaker Truth is laid in the heart, not in the head, and we too must be prepared to undertake the necessary internal work, our own journey of the heart.

For the metaphor of the circumcised heart captures the Quaker sense that beyond our words and our intentions, beyond outwardly doing the right thing, we need to be in right relationship – with our personal Inner Clerk, with the intense power of God, and with the community around us to whom we feel bound. Such right relationship is not a matter of words, or even of deeds. It is a matter of being entire, complete, as a tree is wholly a tree, albeit root, trunk, bough, branch and leaf. With such complete integrity, entire wholeness, all actions flow from a state of ease and inner rest and poise. Acting from this condition, from this calm and balanced centre, all work is then Spirit-led activity. Our work as human beings is to align ourselves with blessed purposiveness, so that the outward work of our hands is the result of the inner work of our heart.

My own story

It is clear to me that on our spiritual paths we are obliged to learn, relearn and unlearn: learn and relearn to live abundantly in the life we have been so freely offered, and unlearn unproductive habits of thought and ways of seeing which hinder our growth as human beings, and hamper our spiritual searching. Some of those things will be products of our early training and cultural conditioning. Since I am trying to share my spiritual experience, and not a set of generalities, I offer a short account of where I started my life journey.

I was born in 1949 in the industrial heartland of South Yorkshire, an area of coal-mining and steel-making. My father's occupation was a labourer, and all of my mother's family worked in coal and steel. Like many in my generation, I was the first in my family history to go to university. My father was what we called then 'deaf and dumb'. My mother was somewhat deaf, had a speech impediment, and what would now be called learning difficulties. My father was considerably older than my mother. He died aged forty-nine, when

I was five. Our family was immediately plunged into bread-and-dripping poverty, and circumstances with which my mother, as a young widow, could barely cope. Later in the 1950s, my mother caused a scandal by having a man in the house she was not married to. He himself was intellectually and emotionally limited. When they did eventually marry, he hated me with a malevolent intensity, my brother marginally less.

Being the older child meant that I was taken under the wing of my grandparents. In fairy tale fashion they lived in a cottage in a wood. I spent many hours walking to and from their cottage, often unaccompanied. In my later journaling, as part of my process of convincement, I found myself writing this:

> I walk through the woods to my grandparents' cottage. I know I am loved. I am lost in the experience. I have no recollection of that journey, that particular visit, but only the experience which fills me with awe, wonder and great joy.

> It is summer. The wood is warm and dark. The sun shines through the leaves above me. Time has ceased, time is of no importance. I am lost in the wonder of being. I am at one with the world.

> Bathed in joy, bathed in love, I wander and I wonder.

Here is the heart of my religious experience, the seed moment of all my subsequent searching, the point at which I became a person founded in the religious life. I am amazed. I have no idea if this incident actually happened. It is not memory, or dream, but some moment of infinite awareness, captured in time, held in apparent memory.

As you might imagine, my early religious training in my home environment was pretty thin gruel. Primary school offered Bible stories, especially Old Testament Bible stories which, much to my amazement, provided potent images in my convincement process. I remember being taken to a Pentecostal church and looking on in awe and something like fear at the ranting preacher. This experience left me with a fear of strong emotion in religious experience. I refused, and still refuse, to believe in the validity of instant conversion, the idea of a saviour, and the concept of vicarious atonement. Any language such as 'blood of the lamb', 'God sacrificed his Son for us', 'needing to be saved' can still raise the hairs on the back of my head. However, at one point I found myself weeping for all those things done to me; all that I had done; all the pain of the world. In Sunday school one day we were asked to raise our hand if we offered ourselves up to Jesus. I do remember feeling obliged to put up my hand up and being called to the front to be prayed over. At the beginning of my convincement process, in 2008, I had the strong sense that I had betrayed this child who had so freely offered his life. In Pendle Hill I had the experience of an American Quaker praying for me and over me. Initially I was embarrassed – this was too reminiscent of unpleasant childhood memories. However, as she thanked God for the meticulous attention paid to our lives, I had the sense that I was encountering Truth.

I failed my Eleven Plus exam, and so was consigned, along with the majority of the children of our area, to the local secondary modern school. As young as I was, in my three and something years in that school, I developed a strong sense of injustice and unfairness. It was not at all the sense that I personally had been treated unfairly, but that the system itself was unjust – it was the sheer waste of humanity implicit in that school system which still appals me after all these years.

Later two English teachers intervened to argue that a small number of us should be transferred to the grammar school section, with its separate buildings and staff. I was immediately in my element. Among other things, in an O level Scripture class, a teacher placed a Bible in my hands and told me to read Matthew, Mark and Luke and I would pass the exam. For eighteen months I sat three times each week reading stories of labourers, vineyards and returning sons. This is the lifeblood of my religious vocabulary today. School life was completed by my conviction in sixth form that I was an atheist, and refusing to study Scripture A Level as a consequence.

My A Level grades were below expectation, but allowed me to scrape into Cardiff University. A different world awaited me. A full grant and summer work meant I had a limited independent income.

Through the passionate teaching of a young enthusiastic lecturer, now a good Friend, I was introduced to works in the mystical tradition. I met Gwyneth, who was to be my wife, and through her met the language and culture of Wales, that still has the capacity to surprise, irritate and intrigue me when I meet it. After university, I became a teacher in a leading comprehensive school in Hertfordshire, but I found life in Britain constricting. I gained a post in an American mission school for boys in southern Turkey and went to Tarsus as a teacher. A year later, Gwyneth and I married and she joined me there.

We loved our simple life together in Tarsus – physically and emotionally set aside from acquisitive consumer society, encountering people who had based their lives on service. I encountered the power of culture to influence our lives. It is not my experience that we are all the same beneath our skin. Just the opposite – family experiences, cultural experiences, life experiences, make us all very different just beneath the skin. We are all caught in the net of history, culture and family, all of these influencing us in ways beyond our awareness. Western thought frames are simply that – a limited perspective on the world. And sometimes these are not effective lenses for seeing God's presence.

A background to this life was the presence of Islam. Running behind memories of sunshine are images of cool mosques, simple and sometimes austere centres of worship. The call to prayer reminded the worshippers that their lives are grounded in Allah, and that he is so great that they must bow down to the ground in awe and fear and trembling. The call to prayer haunts me still, and I thrill to its sound. I am struck at this point in my life not by the differences between Christianity and Islam and variations in belief and ritual, but by the similarities between Islam and Quakerism. They are both religions founded in the desert – one literally so, the other in the desert of the heart. Both are non-credal. In both, worship is as simple and austere as the buildings they worship in. To enter a mosque is to enter a quiet space of great reverence. Later, we encountered Judaism through an unforgettable visit to Jerusalem and making Jewish friends. These experiences showed me that the Christianity I had known to that point was inadequate to contain the complexity of human and religious experience.

Despite its origins in missionary call to service, the school where we worked was at that time a difficult, divided place, and became an opportunity to yet again experience how unpleasant people can be to each other, how awkward to live with, and recalcitrant in dealing with authority; how difficult it is to build, sustain and nurture community. There were plenty of opportunities for misunderstanding, miscommunication and downright bloody-mindedness. In this enforced community, two people stood out. One was a male interim principal. His leadership was a listening one, respectful yet uncompromising in its willingness to challenge aspects of practice which he found unacceptable to community order and well-being. For one year he brought clarity of purpose and clear direction, with a willingness to listen to all. The other was the female librarian, whose home was a haven of hospitality and respite. Her door was literally always open. She demonstrated a seemingly boundless generosity, sharing her records, books and precious coffee. The interim principal embodied a model of leadership which looked to include multiple points of view, where authority was exercised with wisdom and insight; the librarian embodied a generosity of spirit, and welcoming hospitality to all. She was particularly gifted in being able to communicate across the cultural divides which were so markedly apparent. Although completely unrelated to each other, both of them were Quakers. Although this is now many years ago, these two individuals still seem to me to demonstrate some of the qualities I would like others to find in my life; in some way they embody what it is to be Quaker.

On our return home, inspired by these two people whose presence was a source of peace and healing to a riven community, we had a vague awareness that at some point we would want to attend a Quaker meeting. I went back to University to study for a further degree. One evening, in the town library of the small university town of Bangor in North Wales, I found a leaflet "Your first time in a Quaker meeting" and we decided to attend the very next Sunday. We sat in the small hired room up a set of stairs, and within minutes of arriving I heard a voice in my head say "Why have you been travelling the face of this planet? There is no need to journey any more. You are home." From then on, I have always felt at home in the deep silence of a gathered

Quaker meeting. An enduring testimony to my father's presence in my life is that this silence, rather than ritual prayer or song, has always been the most appropriate expression of worship. He showed me that what was true lay beyond mere words. At different times I have imagined this silence in different ways – a deep pool into which I dive, exploring the depths like a diver; an oasis of calm in a busy life into which I sink; a space into which I enter to be with the source of my life – but through all these the silence has remained the place where I come home.

The new life

There are at least two reasons why we may not be persuaded of the way of life evidenced by early Friends. One is that it runs counter to many accounts of human behaviour – some promoted by Christian churches – which present a 'deficit model' of humanity, one based on emphasising shortcomings. George Fox found the same in the churches of his day:

> I said to them, 'If you believe, you are passed from death to life and so from the sin that bringeth death.' They said they believed no such thing, that any could be free from sin while upon the earth.[17]

These beliefs about humanity are intellectual constructs that suggest we are lacking something, or need something extra in order for our existence to be validated: that we need to believe something, or do something, and then we will be worthy of existence. Other, more contemporary models, suggest we are simply the end product of socio-biological forces.

Deeply encoded in the genetic make-up of Quakerism is the belief that, at the heart of the universe, there is good; that life is meaningful; that beyond the immediate pain of experience there is untrammelled joy; that as individuals we are meant to revel in our gifts, delighting in the abundance of who we are; and that, despite the weight of human history, humanity is meant to live in peace.

Another reason why we find it difficult to accept this truth is that many of us have an internal voice which consistently undermines us, constantly telling us that we are unworthy, constantly picking away at our confidence. A great deal of human misery is created by people responding to this inner voice. Sometimes that voice has been placed there by damaging or warping experiences in childhood or adolescence. We can add to the power of that voice, telling ourselves that we never had the right education, the appropriate parenting, or found the life partner we really desired: any one of a number of things which would make us better, more equipped, to face the world. But ultimately this voice is telling us that we are not worthy or lovable as we are. Accessing the loving power at the heart of a meeting for worship can help us into a recognition that this is what Walter Wink describes as the "voice of the slanderer", "the voice that whispers to us, just when we need to marshall all our abilities to perform an important task, 'You're no good, and you never will be any good.' "[18] It is not the voice of that Presence which delights in our unbounding glory, that does not wish to see us diminished in any way, and rejoices when we revel in our gifts.

Early Quakers knew that purity of heart is possible. They were not naïve about the complexity of the task, or the difficulty of the journey when we commit ourselves to such a way of life.

George Fox:
Wait upon God in that which is pure. Though you see your nakedness and barrenness and unfruitfulness… it is the Light that [shows] all this and the Love of God to you.[19]

They were keenly aware of the difficulties of entering and staying in this place, of living out a new reality. They recognised that it could not be achieved simply by desiring it to be so, or by straining after it. It was not a cost-free journey, but involved sacrifice, and some degree of pain.

The modern day mind may have difficulty with pain. Earlier ages, before the widespread use of anaesthetic and antibiotics, were very familiar with pain, since it was the inevitable, often terrible, accompaniment of birth and death. Even today, birth is a not a pain-free process: it is the price to be paid for new life. When we wish to talk of the emotional pain of grief, or loss, we have devised phrases like 'letting go', or 'moving on'. While these words acknowledge that the condition of pain and hurt are not ones to dwell in, the language may make a difficult psychological process seem easy, even effortless. I have no desire to increase the burden of pain in the world, but I think we need to recognise the pain which is an inevitable concomitant of existence, of just being alive.

For to be alive is to grow. And although it seems a natural condition, growth is not always easy – for the plant to grow, a seed must die. When people deliberately seek inner growth with the help of a psychotherapist, they are brought to a point where they can lead more satisfying lives. Such professionals tell us of the pain felt when their clients lay down an inappropriate conceptual model in favour of a more complex cognitive model – one which enables them to live that fuller, richer life.

Early Quakers too knew how difficult it is to let go of those thought frames we have grown up with, the perceptions we have inherited from social conditioning and our own negative experiences – all the things which may inhibit us from seeing reality anew. It is much easier to live in the world of our own social and psychological conditioning, a world where habit, convention or timidity offer prime motivations for behaviour. They knew how difficult it was to prepare oneself for a new reality, where the deepest structures of our inner being, our deepest psyche, are to be founded in love. To get to this inner place is so demanding that Quakers drew on the image of the crucifixion: they talked of 'crucifying the will' and 'going to the cross'.

....

William Penn:
The Cross mystical is that divine grace and power which crosseth the carnal wills of men and gives a contradiction to their corrupt affections... and so may justly be termed the instrument of man's wholly dying to the world, and being made conformable to the will of God.[20]

....

These phrases suggest terrible pain. It is the pain of relinquishing outmoded world views inimical to making loving Presence the bedrock of our existence. But we must remember that the crucifixion was not a story of extinction, but one of complete transformation; not death, but release into a state beyond the world's comprehension. Here is the story of Mary Dyer, condemned to death in 1660 in Massachusetts:

> Thus guarded, she came to the gallows, and being gone up the ladder, some said to her that if she would return [home] she might come down and save her life. To which she replied, "Nay, I cannot, for in obedience to the will of the Lord I came, and in His will I abide faithful to death"... Then one mentioned that she should have said, she had been in Paradise. To which she answered, "Yea, I have been in Paradise these several days."[21]

It is a coming home to that person we truly are. We release those energies deep within ourselves, energies hidden from us in the habits of our usual daily existence; and we also draw on that energy, ever present, in a gathered meeting.

So the spiritual journey is one of healing, mending our internal wounds and righting the perceptions imposed by a culture which is awry. Healing is at the heart of the Quaker world-view because it is at the heart of the Christian world-view. In Mark's gospel the first healing ministry is one of dispossessing a man of the devils which haunt him, prevent him from being whole: we are intended to move towards wholeness.[22] Yet the spiritual path is not simply a therapeutic journey. The Quaker experience is not just about being released from those things which inhibit our growth into life's abundance; it is release for a purpose. Blockages are cleared so that we may be channels for divine light and love. We are freed from timidity, hurt, anxiety and fear so that we may be co-agents in creating the new reality of the Kingdom of God. For some of us, particularly those injured by childhood hurts, that road is long and hard. It is the road of discipleship. It is a road I walk stumblingly. I have to travel the path of healing so that piece by piece, brick by brick, I dismantle the empire of my mind, and plant a garden of the heart; step by step, best as I am guided, I play my part in creating a Kingdom based on love. My role model is early Friends. In their discipleship path, in their talk of crucifixion of the will, they knew that it was not talking of the extinction of self, but fulfilment of themselves as human beings.

This process of following a discipleship path meant that their sole motivation became to 'place themselves in right ordering' with the divine purpose for their lives. They desired to be so in tune with divine purpose that they could hear and recognise their call – the purpose for which each of them had been created. Whatever that work was, they saw themselves as Children of Light, emanating loving presence as they walked over the darkness of the world.

....

James Nayler:
You, the tender plants of my Father, who have suffered thro'
me or with me... in this time of great trial and temptation, the
Almighty God of Love... fulfill your joy with his love, which
you seek after. [23]

....

I think it important that we understand this internal heartwork of early Friends, for it offers us an inheritance of rich possibility today: we in our turn can make the necessary inward re-ordering which allows us to be Children of Light, founded in love. In this search for our inward clarity of heart and mind, we are not seeking to adopt an abstract model of perfection by which we can judge ourselves, for we will inevitably fail. We can accept that we have been created to be God's instruments, with all our human flaws, flecks and imperfections.

I am often moved at Yearly Meeting when I read Testimonies to the Grace of God in the lives of Friends:

Our custom of writing testimonies to the grace of God as shown in the lives of Friends provides us with a wealth of material showing ordinary Friends living out their faith from day to day. These testimonies show us that, whatever our circumstances, God can be present with us, and they encourage us each to be faithful to our own calling.[24]

The pictures which emerge will often be clear-sighted about a Friend's sharpness of tongue, irascibility, impatience with poor observance of Quaker discipline: the pictures which emerge are not of saints, walking six inches above the ground wrapped in some ethereal mist yet surrounded by glowing light. They are of human beings, struggling to be faithful, with all the gifts and characteristics which they have been given to manage in this world.

Unlike early Friends, we have great riches opened up to us by our greater understanding of the mind and its relationship to our emotional health. They may have lived in very different times, so that they did not know of psychotherapy: but they knew the slow rhythmic plod of the plough, the regular sound of butter being churned, the hammering of hot iron on anvil. I do not think it is too fanciful of me to think of these as offering possibilities for the deep inward searching of the type we are describing – the searching that leads an inner reorientation of our way of being, based on a sense of loving purpose for our lives. We cannot reach this place using the power of our minds, for it is beyond the level of our surface thinking. It involves us in work on our hearts. It will also involve us in some work on our minds, and the way we see things, in that we need to fully assent to this condition, want to live in it, and turn our minds to how we might get there.[25] But just as in the Orthodox tradition a worshipper will gaze upon an icon in order to get to the space beyond the surface image, so we must penetrate far beyond mere thought, the world constructed by our minds, if we are to engage with our deepest self, our Inner Clerk, and thereby with our Higher Power. As we move towards wholeness we find that completeness, that integrity, for which we were intended.

We are not exactly sure of the processes early Friends used to enter this mystical communion. Following his theological study of early Friends' writings, Rex Ambler devised Experiment with Light as a Quaker practice based on early Friends' discoveries in worship.[26] Those who follow Experiment with Light say they have discovered a clear connection between that practice and those of early Friends.

For those of us who have engaged with this process, it offers a sense of rich authenticity. However, we can recognise that there is not just one path to this inner place, this internal deep space; rather that many gates of entry are offered, only some of which will speak to us in our own unique individuality. For example, I have very little capability for manual dexterity, so for me it is not the path of building or making which is part of the fabric of my being: these are inadequate spiritual tools in my hands. My core practices are journaling, and sitting quietly with my breath. As well as Experiment with Light, I have found an extremely powerful source of insight in Appleseed, which was a Quaker travelling ministry conducted through the experience of art,[27] and in a process called Life Writing For Transformation, developed as a means of gaining clarity and enriching an individual's life.[28]

Whatever way we choose (or rather chooses us), if we follow it with patience and persistence we will find it a path of healing, towards inner wholeness. As an athlete seeks to perform at a level which sometimes surpasses our expectation of human performance, so we can prepare ourselves to be amazed where we might be taken by dint of regular practice – a practice which might be known as prayer.

In this spirit of prayer, early Friends intended to be so in tune, 'in right ordering with divine purpose', that they could hear and recognise their call – that purpose for which they and they alone had been created.

....

William Dewsbury:
I joyfully entered prisons as palaces, telling mine enemies to
hold me there as long as they could... for they could keep me
there no longer than the appointed time of my God.[29]

....

This calling took many forms: to leave hearth and plough, to visit the Great Turk, to build a boat, to write the constitution of Pennsylvania – it simply meant undertaking the internal work so that they might do the external work which creates the Kingdom of God.

In 2011 Gwyneth and I enjoyed a term as resident Friends at Pendle Hill in Pennsylvania.[30] Generally, Americans seem to be a people more open to God – unapologetically they will speak of God and invoke his presence. The sense that we can open our hearts to God, that we can legitimately expect to be transformed, runs through much of American Quakerism.

This was the context in which I had three personal revelations. The first was a vision of great compassion in the universe. The second was the discovery of deep burning anger at social injustice. The third was a class in which I encountered what helped me reconcile these claims on my heart.

The vision came in meeting for worship one day. I had the sense of God as an actual person, looking down upon our single solitary planet, the blue planet, floating in the void, seeing this great seething mass of humanity, striving, relentlessly striving. God was looking down upon this world, looking down upon all us humans, each struggling to do the best we can with the bits of flint in our hearts – the unredeemed stories of our loss, our pain, our suffering, and each acting out the best they can be in their circumstances – and God was weeping over this world, his world – weeping for his creation.

The great and burning anger was intimately bound up with my political view of the world, anger at the injustice of it all – that so many had so much, and so many more had so little. This pattern of injustice is historical and worldwide: workers slaved in factories in the nineteenth century to accrue the capital we live on today; the fruits of my affluent Western way of life, where I enjoy so much, are funded by some little child in India, Pakistan or Malaysia, who works for a pittance, and is permanently hungry. I had not realised just how much incandescent rage was at the core of my being. We humans had taken a beautiful planet, and created systems where most of its inhabitants do not have enough to eat, and where women and children can be traded as easily as carcasses of meat.

In encountering this deep anger, I was also given the means to hold it to the Light. I undertook a class where we were asked to look at the entire flower of our being – not just the outer branches, but the stem, and the deepest roots which feed us. In sessions which were deeply uncomfortable to my white, educated self, we were led by our African American facilitator in dance, song, and exercises which encouraged us to probe our deepest being. The point of the class was to show us that we need to be integrated, entire, whole, from our deepest roots to the image we present to the world: in the words of our teacher in Black American idiom, 'Who we say we be' needs to be related to 'Who we be' at our deepest levels of existence. And we were shown how this question is deeply political, in the sense that we are caught up in society where there are power structures and relationships based on secular power.

The politics of early Friends

When I was first discovering Friends, I was often told stories of Quakers refusing to doff their hats, or persisting in using 'thee' and 'thy' to all and sundry – but not the significance of this for myself or my time. I believe it is for us to rediscover and live out their truths in our age.

Firstly, early Friends were a marginal people. The very first Quakers were from the northern upland regions, a poor, neglected area of the country. Although drawn from middling ranks, their diatribes against the power structures of the day made them despised as 'dregs of the common people'. Both geographically and socially they were people who lived on the margins of Britain.

....

Francis Howgill
[We] were reckoned, in the north part of England, even as the outcasts of Israel, and as men destitute of the great knowledge, which some seemed to enjoy.[31]

....

This teaches me that we do not need to be afraid of being a marginal people. During the next generation, our world is going to see huge changes impelled by our way of life and its impact on our planet. It is not from the mainstream that answers will come.

The lives of early Quakers expressed the elemental simplicity of a desert people – they dressed in simple clothes of grey, insisted on simple speech with each other, and eschewed the elaborate courtesies of sophisticated urban dwellers. Their meeting houses were bare, elemental, stripped down in order to create the desert experience of purification and renewal.

Isaac Penington:
I met with some writings of this people called Quakers, which I cast a slight eye upon and disdained as falling very short of that wisdom, light, life and power which I had been longing for... [But] when I came, I felt the presence and power of the Most High among them, and words of truth...[32]

If we do not need to fear the desert, neither do we need to fear our desert experiences – those times when we are lost, alone and stumbling; those times when we feel our lives are simply a barren emptiness.

James Nayler:
There is a spirit which I feel that delights to do no evil nor to revenge any wrong... I found it alone, being forsaken. I have fellowship therein with them who lived in dens and desolate places in the earth, who through death obtained this resurrection and eternal holy life.[33]

We can trust that our lives are meant to shine. As the love of God streams across the desolate emptiness of the universe for each and every one of us, so our lives are meant to shine forth his Light. We are his hands, and our work is transforming his planet so that it more nearly resembles the Kingdom he wishes us to inherit – not the conflicted world of lust for possession, power and greed which we human beings create.

Early Friends taught me about the nature of power. They had recently emerged from a civil war, with all the suffering that involves, in which little was left of the society they once knew. About one third of the men who went on to be Quaker had fought in the war. The expectations they had had for creating a better world through warfare had come to nought. War is a doomed and hopeless affair. Quakers showed there is another way. It was the way of the desolation of the will: the willingness to relinquish an addiction to certainty and the desire to impose one's will on others, obliging others to act and believe as we do.

As a consequence of making this journey, being faithful to their call, Quakers produced the Peace Testimony in 1660, in a difficult set of circumstances.

> Our principle is, and our practices have always been, to seek peace, and ensue it, and to follow after righteousness and the knowledge of God, seeking the good and welfare, and doing that which tends to the peace of all. All bloody principles and practices we do utterly deny, with all outward wars, and strife, and fightings with outward weapons, for any end, or under any pretence whatsoever, and this is our testimony to the whole world. That spirit of Christ by which we are guided is not changeable, so as once to command us from a thing as evil, and again to move unto it; and we do certainly know, and so testify to the world, that the spirit of Christ which leads us into all Truth will never move us to fight and war against any man with outward weapons, neither for the kingdom of Christ, nor for the kingdoms of this world.

> And as for the kingdoms of this world, we cannot covet them, much less can we fight for them, but we do earnestly desire and wait, that by the word of God's power and its effectual operation in the hearts of men the kingdoms of this world may become the kingdoms of the Lord and of his Christ, that he might rule and reign in men by his spirit and truth, that thereby all people, out of all different judgments and professions might be brought into love and unity with God and one with another, and that they might all come to witness the prophet's words, who said, 'Nation shall not lift up sword

against nation, neither shall they learn war any more' (Isaiah 2:4; Micah 4:3).[34]

If we are not careful, we can today interpret the Testimony as a clever response to a political reality pressing on Friends at the time. But the reality is that that commitment to peace had long been made earlier in the hearts and lives of Quaker men, when they turned their lives over to God. Time and time again they allowed themselves to be beaten, stoned, hit – and refused to retaliate. Nayler blessed the man who was to bore a red hot iron through his tongue. They were indeed fighting a battle – they were fighting the Lamb's War – but they were warriors for Truth who refused to use the weapons of the world. By confronting their own darkness, Quakers were well placed to confront external darkness – the hierarchical, oppressive systems which preachers, hat honour and social structures represented.

....

George Fox:
Your sufferings will reach to the prisoned [Light], which the persecutor prisons in himself.[35]

....

But their own hearts and minds were clear; because they had overcome their internal oppression, Quakers were freed of the need to oppress others.

What does this mean for us today? Firstly, it means we have to be prepared to relinquish our very human addiction to a sense of personal control over our lives, recognising that such a sense is an illusion of our own making: we have no control over what happens to us. It is an understandable human need to require certainty: it helps us feel safe in a demanding and uncertain world. But as Quakers our work is to discern a greater will, not impose human constructions and values on situations. This might lead us on a path which is more complex and demanding than anything we could possibly imagine for ourselves. Often the path is not clear. Very often all we can do is take the next faithful step. But we can be sure that as we move towards wholeness, we are releasing the love of God onto the planet.

Secondly, we can learn that, as Quakers, we have no need to fear an assured Quaker confidence, for it is of a different order than the certainty offered by the world. In the religious sphere, as in so much else, there is a human desire for certainty. Dogma is simply such a projection of the human need for certainty. But Quaker assurance is not that of imposing a mental construct on the world – it is a confidence which comes from discerning an unfolding plan, playing our part as our way emerges from the deep silence.

And thirdly, we can understand that it is for us to challenge the easy assumptions and common complacencies of the world around us: ours is not only to comfort the afflicted, but to afflict the comfortable.

For me these understandings are not messages from an older people, needing to rest in some Museum of Quaker History – they offer dynamic, exciting vibrant Quaker truths for today. The historic legacy of the Quaker tradition is that our lives are meant to be lived as part of a divine pattern, to which we ourselves must submit. We may never fully comprehend the total pattern, which is why our actions must never outrun our leadings, but we can participate actively, with full authenticity and rich bodied experience, by trying to listen to divine will and seeking our intended purpose.

Recapturing the vision

This means that we can seek the work for which we have been created, and expect to find it. That work will vary for each one of us, and it may not be immediately apparent. The earlier we begin to prepare ourselves, the sooner we can expect to find it. It will vary according to our own gifts, and may change over time as we grow in the spirit. Invariably it will involve a sea-change in our desires and passions so that they may be used for God driven ends. In my own case I found at root that, despite all appearances to the contrary, I was a very angry person. My anger, when it did not spill out on those who are very near and dear to me, was directed at those persons who create and support systems of economic injustice in the world. I have discovered that it is not that I should never be angry, but that my anger should not be directed at persons, for they are as much children of God as I am; but it does need to be directed at the root causes of injustice. I needed strength not to live in my burning anger, or inflict it on the world, but have it transmuted into awareness and righteous action. I await the call for my next step.

The sacrifices which are an inextricable part of that movement to which we are invited will vary according to who we are: that complex of genetic make-up, emotional disposition, the nature and extent of our life experiences and our response to them – which all contribute to that image of divinity which is our life. Some of us may need to seek long and diligently before we can find such awareness. We need to learn to be patient. But once we are on the path, once we commit ourselves, then movement towards wholeness is as certain as the sunrise.

And as we move towards wholeness, so we are released into the present moment.

....

George Fox
Oh, be faithful! Look not back, nor be too forward, further than ye have attained; for ye have no time but this present time: therefore, prize your time for your souls' sake.[36] *(From a letter to his parents in 1652.)*

....

As human beings, we have a propensity to dwell in the past. Negative experiences, especially those of a searing kind, tend to be incorporated into a life narrative, which is why I have shared my own with you. Consciously or unconsciously, I allowed the past to dominate the present. Some of us have been hurt badly by experiences in a traditional Christian church. Because of this, it is quite possible that we came to Quakers because their way seems not to be constrained by particular language; indeed we may begin to resent and reject any form of Christian language as an affront to our condition. In this, and countless other ways, we are allowing ourselves to be dominated by past experience, not responding to the Life which is opening up before us as each moment unfolds. I write as one who has had had to recognise that a narrative formed in a poverty stricken childhood and subsequent life decisions was holding me back from acknowledging and appreciating the abundance of Life on offer, if I could but see it. I have made life-long attempts to find a rational, sensible, acceptable understanding of the world. But, as I have come home, it is the words of early Friends which express the truth I have encountered and the power of my experience.

As we have a propensity to re-live the past, so we have a capacity to be anxious for the future, and all it holds. At each moment of history, people are born at a time of frightening change. At each point, there is much to create a picture of impending danger and difficulty. My own life was marked by the death of my father: I am constantly aware of the fragility of human life, and how at any moment our circumstances can change – human life hangs by a very fine thread. Just as our tongues have the capacity to process a number of apparently contradictory tastes – sweet, bitter, salt, sour – so we are designed to encounter a variety of immediate experiences. Some of these have the power to be utterly destructive of our capacity to trust, and to reciprocate love. At its surface, human life is full of ambiguity, paradox and ambivalence. This does not contradict our capacity for 'deep structure' experiences: we can commit ourselves in our hearts to adopting a trusting assurance, recognising that there is a fundamental movement which belies the surface pattern:

> Take heed, dear Friends, to the promptings of love and truth
> in your hearts. Trust them as the leadings of God whose
> Light shows us our darkness and brings us to new life.[37]

This is not easy, for we do not live in a religious age. Britain, unlike say America or Iran, is not a religious country.[38] In addition, particularly we in the West are locked into thought frames which require the authenticity of objective truth based on the experimentation of the scientist. But we need not expect our religious truths to operate in the same dimension as scientific truth, even though they both play out in the material world. Over time, humanity adds to its information base, and the stock of understandings; over time, we incorporate this information into our ideas about ourselves and how the universe works, so that in each age we develop a different world view accepted as the model of the universe. Today we seek the certainties of science, even as science reaches into poetry to express its quest for its version of truth. We find it difficult to trust our experience of the divine, and instead seek the assurance of intellectual certainty. We are addicted to *logos*, when we could accept, difficult as it is in our current age, the power of *mythos* – narrative, metaphor and poetry.

The divine economy and community

My own experience is that for many years of my life I was part of this confusion, of living in Babylon, living by my mind, and by what I thought were my own energies, gifts and talents. Although I could hear an alternative world order, it was as the sound of children in a playground very far away, faintly carried on the breeze, having little to do with my circumstance in the real world. It has been a long time in coming, but I now recognise myself as an expression of God's infinite love for this planet. My capacities, my experiences, my strengths and vulnerabilities have all been given to me, and framed as part of an infinite pattern. This at once makes my life supremely important, and of no significance. My life is important in that it is through me that God's love finds one unique expression in this world, mediated through my flesh and bone and material work. So I must tend carefully my physical, emotional, psychological and spiritual well-being to ensure that I am a capable instrument for God's purpose. I am required to develop a sustainable economy for myself, in order to participate fully in the divine economy.

I discovered something of this when I served on a Quaker central committee. The sense of shared purpose and fellowship which sprang from our gathering together four times each year was an object lesson in the creation of community. We took time, even in packed weekends, to learn of each other's current life situation, and any particular joys and sorrows which occupied our mind. We shared each other's spiritual journeys, and were not afraid to recognise each other's gifts, seeking to utilise them in the work which occupied us between meetings. In meeting my fellow committee members, and many of our staff, my life was enriched, and my sense of what it is to be Quaker was deepened and enriched by their love, of each other and the work, their care for each other, and their deep sense of worship. I met again the spirit which I had sensed in the two Quaker staff at the college in Tarsus.

....

George Fox:
And this is the word of the Lord God to you all, and a charge to you all in the presence of the living God: be patterns, be examples in all countries, places, islands, nations, wherever you come, that your carriage and life may preach among all sorts of people, and to them; then you will come to walk cheerfully over the world, answering that of God in every one.[39]

....

We are called to be patterns and examples. Yet if I were to stress and strain in order to live up to some ideal of behaviour, some blueprint of how I should live in the world, my life would not be a testimony to God's love in action. Instead of living out a dynamic relationship, I would be living in accordance with a mental construction of my own devising – it would be a form of idolatry. Idolatry of any kind – of earlier generations, of a form of words, a particular person or idea – warps our judgement, rendering us incapable of responding fully to the joys and stresses of each moment in which we are living.

Nor can we achieve it alone, as the early Friends knew. Their community was not one of individuals grouping together to pursue a common interest.

When early Friends affirmed the priesthood of all believers it was seen as an abolition of the clergy; in fact it is an abolition of the laity. All members are part of the clergy and have the clergy's responsibility for the maintenance of the meeting as a community.[40]

It was rather that in abolishing the laity, they bound themselves to each other in a way which had no parallel in the secular world. We sometimes use the metaphor of 'our Quaker family', meaning a close loving relationship. But the early Quaker community was formed to make manifest to the world that living presence which they encountered in the depths of silent meeting.

Robert Barclay:
When I came into the silent assemblies of God's people, I felt
a secret power among them, which touched my heart; and as
I gave way unto it I found the evil weakening in me and the
good raised up.[41]

Their words of ministry, their tracts and pamphlets, gave voice to that living presence; their actions embodied God's presence on earth. Their community had no need for the elaborate social niceties of the day; it recognised that Friends were drawn together by motivations which were not those of 'the world'.

They were under no illusions about the demanding, sometimes difficult and painful path into a condition where they lived in the present moment, responding with great joy to whatever situation befell them, knowing they were taking their place in a divine pattern in which they were utterly beloved Children of the Light. They were aware too of the challenges of staying in this place:

George Fox:
Friends, whatever ye are addicted to, the tempter will come
in that thing; and when he can trouble you, then he gets
advantage over you, and then you are gone. Stand still in that
which is pure, after ye see yourselves; and then mercy comes
in. After thou seest thy thoughts, and the temptations, do
not think, but submit; and then power comes. Stand still
in that which shows and discovers; and then doth strength
immediately come. And stand still in the Light, and submit
to it, and the other will be hushed and gone; and then content
comes.[42]

We do not feel comfortable with this language today. We tend to dismiss as superstitious, childish or uneducated any talk of the devil, demons or spirits. As Walter Wink says, at dinner parties "if you want to bring all talk to a halt in shocked embarrassment, every eye riveted on you, try mentioning angels, or demons or the devil"[43]. However, once again, if we see beyond the surface words of what Fox said, I think we can find considerable help for our own condition. For this is not the voice of theoretical understanding. It is the voice of a man who has seen himself whole, who knows his own temptations – and for a man who possesses the great personal charisma of George Fox those temptations can be many and manifold – and who also knows the peace which comes from resting in a power greater than his own.

If, for a moment, instead of seventeenth-century language we translate through the prism of twentieth-century psychological insight, then it seems to me that this is a very clear, psychologically acute recognition. We often see addictions in terms of an external agency such as drink, drugs or sex. The remarkable insight in this passage is that our addictions can be diverse and numerous – they are part of our 'shadow' which we all carry, unseen, unrecognised, but which can emerge in our actions leading us away from a life of love and peace. Just as we are framed for a particular purpose, and will receive our experience of Presence in a manner specific to us, so our addictions – those things which take us from living in a dynamic awareness of loving Presence – are also specific to us. They may be addictions within our culture, but they appeal to each of us in a unique way. Where we carry unrecognised grief, hurt or pain – unhealed wounds – we are likely to act from this place, and bring pain to others. For it is precisely in those parts where we carry unhealed wounds that we are also untransformed: where we still cast our own dark shadow on the world.

For a long time I was addicted to a life story which consisted of failure: an endless, repeated internal DVD replaying missed opportunities, poor decisions, and outright failures. 'What if' and 'If only' was a chorus I was very familiar with. On and on and on… An interminable laceration of myself for mistakes, poor decisions and misjudgements along the way. No wonder there was little space for spirit in my life. And it is so easy for me to slip back into this place.

When I allow myself to become tired, when life offers unanticipated and unexpected challenges, when I have not been undertaking my daily practice, then I can so easily find myself slipping back into poor habits of sloppy thinking and casual responses – acting from long established routine rather than an active loving Centre carefully nurtured by loving patience. George Fox tells us here that it is a necessary part of our transformation, our living in right relationship, that these hidden drivers at the core of our being are also subject to the Light.

Early Friends were utterly familiar with their human condition, knowing they had to strengthen and assist each other. But they had considerable confidence because they had a role model who had trod this path before them: that of Jesus in the Gospels. In his being called, they could recognise that they could be called; in his desert temptations, they recognised their own difficulties in following a faithful path; and in his utter faithfulness, even unto death, they recognised that this was possible for us too.

....

James Nayler, to the magistrates in 1652:
If I cannot witness Christ nearer than Jerusalem, I shall have
no benefit by him; but I own no other Christ but that who
witnessed a good confession before Pontius Pilate; which
Christ I witness suffering in me now.[44]

....

For those of us who cannot see Jesus except through the spectacles provided by other churches, we might want to note that Jesus did not proclaim himself the Messiah. The term he used in the gospels to describe himself is Son of Man. A modern day translation for this phrase is "the Human One"[45]. His journey is one into his own humanity. The Christian path as understood by early Quakers is not about escaping the human condition, or having a simple road map through life which elides complexity, skates over difficulty or makes light of suffering – it is living a human life in all its fullness, richness and glory. Given that it is a human life, it will inevitably include periods of difficulty, doubt, darkness and even death, just as the life of Jesus did. There is no final answer to the mystery of the human condition. But the Quaker answer, however provisional and hesitant, has a delight in life, an acknowledgement of the richness and complexity of human experience, and a wholehearted responsive affirmation to the world and all it offers. It sets a lodestar by which I chart my course.

However we phrase it, we can be transformed, individually and collectively. Our hearts can be cleared; we can live at peace with ourselves and our neighbours; we can become bearers of light for the power which energises a gathered meeting. We can live in transformed community. It will be a recognisably human community, and conflict will exist – yet will not prevail. The purpose of this community is to exemplify and manifest the Kingdom, so that others may see a model of the Kingdom here on earth. We walk over this world, its obvious darkness, pain and sorrow, not untouched, but not caught up in its miasma of destruction; resting in God's love we can be patterns and examples which call out that of God in everyone.

I have tried to indicate that my position in the Society changed radically because of my own experiences, and finding these placed in context by the important spiritual truths early Friends offered. I think it important that we do not treat early Friends with either the trite sentimentality of nostalgia, or idolatrous adulation. But nor should we dismiss them as irrelevant. We have to tell their story as accurately as we can. We can recognise and marvel that they were quite ordinary people, born at an extraordinary time, who discovered truths in the depths of their experience of encounter; truths based on a profound sympathy and understanding of the human condition. Who they were as a people helps me not only appreciate the rich heritage we enjoy as Quakers, but deepens my understanding and enriches my faith.

They offer me a vision of what the Society of Friends might yet become: a vibrant community where we bring our whole selves in order to be made whole; where we share with each other the difficult aspects of our journey, as well as the joys and the affirmations we find together; where our lives are made accountable to and for each other; in which we support and uphold each other as each of us strives towards that inner space where love can become our first motion; where each of us works to turn ourselves over to the Light, that power, which has the capacity to transform us. And where people observing our patience with each other in our daily round might say in surprise and wonder, as was said of the early Christians, "See how these Quakers love each other"[46].

Bibliography
Works referred to in the text

Ambler, Rex. *Light to live by: An exploration in Quaker spirituality.* London: Quaker Books, 2002.

Brown, Elizabeth, and Alec Davison, eds. *Journeying the heartlands: Exploring spiritual practices of Quaker worship.* London: The Kindlers, 2009.

Cadbury, Henry J. *Narrative papers of George Fox.* Richmond, IN: Friends United Press, 1972.

Cook, Chris, and Brenda Clifft-Heales. *Images and Silence* (Swarthmore Lecture). London: Quaker Home Service, 1992.

Cronk, Sandra. *Dark Night Journey: Inward re-patterning toward a life centered in God.* Wallingford, PA: Pendle Hill, 1991.

Fox, George, ed. John L. Nickalls. *The Journal of George Fox: a revised edition.* Cambridge University Press, 1952; repr. (with minor corrections) 1975. Philadelphia and London: Philadelphia Yearly Meeting and Quaker Books, 2005.

Fox, George. *The works of George Fox* [8 volumes; reprint of 1831 edition]. State College, Pennsylvania: New Foundation/George Fox Fund, 1990.

Guiton, Gerard. *The early Quakers and the Kingdom of God: Peace testimony and revolution.* San Francisco: Inner Light Books, 2012.

Kelly, Thomas R. *A testament of devotion.* New York: Harper, 1941; repr. 1992.

Kelly, Thomas R. *The eternal promise.* New York: Harper & Row, 1966; repr. Richmond, IN: Friends United Press, 2006.

Myers, Ched. *Binding the strong man: A political reading of Mark's story of Jesus.* New York: Orbis Books, 2008.

Nayler, James. *A collection of sundry books epistles and papers,* edited by George Whitehead. London: J. Sowle, 1716.

Nayler, James. *The works of James Nayler* [in four volumes]. Glenside, PA: Quaker Heritage Press, 2003–2009; also available online at www.qhpress.org.

Penington, Isaac, ed. R. Melvin Keiser & Rosemary Moore. *Knowing the mystery of life within: Selected writings of Isaac Penington in their historical and theological context.* London: Quaker Books, 2005.

Penn, William. *No cross, no crown: A discourse showing the nature and discipline of the holy cross of Christ.* [First published 1669]. York: Sessions Book Trust, 1981.

Putnam, Robert, and David E. Campbell. *American Grace: How Religion Divides and Unites Us.* New York: Simon & Schuster, 2010.

Quaker faith & practice: The book of Christian discipline of the Yearly Meeting of the Religious Society of Friends (Quakers) in Britain. London: Britain Yearly Meeting, 1995; rev. fourth edition, 2009.

Tertullian. *Apology, De Spectaculis*; with an English translation by T.R. Glover. (Loeb Classical Library 250). Harvard University Press, 1931.

Woolman, John, ed. Phillips P. Moulton. *The journal and major essays.* Richmond, IN: Friends United Press, 1989.

Wink, Walter. *Unmasking the powers: The invisible forces that determine human existence.* Philadelphia: Fortress Press, 1986.

Wink, Walter. *The powers that be: Theology for a new millennium.* New York: Doubleday, 1999.

Journey into Life

Responding to and resonating with
the 2013 Swarthmore Lecture

Introduction

As Quakers, stories are important to us: in our Quaker tradition which rests on experience, rather than abstractions, our stories are a way of making manifest our experience. There are all manner of stories in our religious society: of Quakers in the past; of our meetings and our religious life together; of the stories we tell with our own lives. These stories have the capacity to inspire us, challenge us, humble us and guide us, if we let them. Just as Testimonies to the lives of dead Friends hold up the story of a life, so stories of our lives become living testimonies. We can find inspiration from each other.

The following activities enable us to reflect on the story of one Friend's life told in the lecture and to tell our own stories in an atmosphere of safe listening.

Purpose of the activities

The following activities are designed to enable Friends to look at the Swarthmore Lecture in order to find the Light in their own lives. The intention is to find those points where our lives resonate with the text in order to help us see the Light in our lives, and in the community in which we worship together. It is important that we approach and encounter our lives and spiritual journeys without that sometimes deafening voice of the slanderer, that internal inner critic who diminishes us. In order to do this, it is essential we lay aside the voice of the outer critic. We do this not to ignore what is difficult or demanding or negative, but to allow us to view things with a soft focus, as though perhaps approaching them for the first time, seeing them with loving eyes. This means putting to one side, temporarily, points where we may disagree or find fault, focusing only on these points where we feel ourselves to be in harmony with the text.

Initially the activities pay close attention to the text, in order for Friends to then pay attention to their own lives and experience, and what they find there. This approach may be different from people's previous experience of group work or creative listening, but it has proved to be a valuable approach if the guidelines are adhered to.

The text of the lecture can be read with a number of 'lenses', or from different perspectives. These different readings might lend themselves to work with different groups of people, for different purposes. The first section – for individuals or close spiritual friends/companions – suggests working at a level of personal intimacy not required by the other sections.

Using these activities

Though the guidelines are quite strict, the activities are designed to be used very flexibly. There are activities for individuals, small groups (twos, threes or fours) and larger groups (with a focus on whole meetings). The activities have been designed to be done with minimal equipment. Participants may wish to bring pens and paper/notebooks for their own notes, where equipment is needed this is specified.

Although divided into three sections you may wish to spread the activities over more than three sessions, going at a pace that suits the group. We recommend that each session runs for a maximum of 90 minutes.

Guidance for facilitators and group members

In undertaking these activities it is important that all participants come with heart and mind prepared. It is probably helpful for some members of each group to be designated as 'facilitators', perhaps on a rotating basis, to guide the group through the process, keep an eye on time and 'hold' the group. It may be appropriate for them to decide the order in which the group approaches the activities, the methods used and the framework in which the group will work. Everyone else should not come expecting to be directed or merely be guided through the process but to engage fully and wholeheartedly. As Friends we do not have a separated priesthood, and all have the clergy's responsibility for the maintenance of the meeting as a community. Similarly in our groups, we all hold the responsibility to work collaboratively in order for the group to work together, enabling us to reflect on our spiritual journeys and helping us see the Light in our lives, and in the community in which we worship together.

In **preparation** for your session **read the introduction and purpose** above which sets out the intention for these activities.

Discuss and agree how the group will work together

In small groups and whole meeting groups all members of the group should have a chance to share and one or two persons should not dominate the spoken contributions (and this includes the facilitators). It may be helpful to state a few general guidelines, which are the foundation for the approaches below.

- **Come to the group with as much of ourselves as possible**. This means two things: to be as present as we can be (which may differ depending on the day, or the time of day or what else is happening) and to bring all of whom we are – our joys and successes, our fears and failings. You may pass if you do not wish to speak to the topic or answer a question.
- **Presume welcome and extend welcome**. We support each other's participation and growth by giving and receiving hospitality.
- **No fixing**. No fixing, counselling, setting straight. Your tutor

and fellow participants are there to support you through your journey rather than to set you straight.

- **When the going gets tough, turn to wonder.** When you find yourself reacting harshly, disagreeing with another, becoming judgemental or becoming defensive, ask questions like "I wonder what my reaction teaches me about myself".
- **Speak for self.** Using 'I' statements, speak your truth in a way that respects the truths of others. Speak for a second time only after others have had a chance to speak once.
- **Listen with 'soft eyes'.** Listen to others with eyes of compassion and understanding.
- **Trust and learn from silence.** Silence is a rare gift in our busy world. Allow silence to be another member of the group. Leave silence between speakers.
- **Observe confidentiality.** The main issue in relation to confidentiality is agreeing how exceptions will work in practice. There will be times when people share ideas, approaches or experiences that are helpful to others. It is part of our Quaker tradition that we share and learn from each other within the Priesthood of all believers. However it is important to respect individuals' personal stories. A general principle is that it is okay to share ideas but not personal stories. The following is a suggestion which you can adapt to suit your group.
    - Everything shared in pairs/small groups is confidential to those present *except for* agreed things which may be reported to the main group and discussed during the session.
    - Everything shared in the whole group stays in the group and is not discussed outside the session *except for* agreed things which may be discussed outside the session between course members only.
- **Accept imperfection.** In ourselves and in others.

Beginning your session

We suggest that every session starts with a reminder of what the session is designed to enable; your introduction could include the following points.

- The intention of these activities is to find those points where our lives resonate with the text in order to help us see the Light in our lives, and in the community in which we worship together.
- It is important that we approach and encounter our lives and spiritual journeys without the voice of the inner critic who diminishes us. To do this we must lay aside the voice of the outer critic.
- This is not to ignore what is difficult or demanding or negative, but to allow us to view things with loving eyes.
- This means putting to one side, temporarily, points where we may disagree or find fault, focusing only on these points where we feel ourselves to be in harmony with the text.
- Initially the activities pay close attention to the text, in order for Friends to then pay attention to their own lives and experience, and what they find there.

Approaches for Group Work[1]

Creative listening

Participants take turns around the circle, giving each a chance to say something on the topic. Limiting the responses to 2–3 minutes may be useful so that the entire time is not used in this one **go-round**.
- Each offering is given without expectation of questions or comments from others in the group.
- To help share time equally, **a watch** may be held by the person who has just spoken and handed to the next speaker at the end of the allotted time.

Creative listening may also be used for **longer contributions** in which case people may contribute in any order. Here are two suggestions to encourage equal participation:
- **Talking stick**. An object, such as a shell, smooth pebble or pine cone is picked up by a speaker who must not be interrupted while holding it. The object can be picked up by anyone for their turn after it has been replaced in the centre of the circle.

---

1 Adapted with permission from *Hearts & Minds Prepared Facilitator Handbook*, published by Woodbrooke Quaker Study Centre 2003.

Some Native North American groups call it the "talking stick". This method is usually most effective when linked with periods of silent worship between contributions.

- **Stones or tokens**. Try giving 2–3 stones or other small objects to each person, each "worth" two minutes. After a minute or so at the start, anyone may toss one into the middle of the circle to signify they are ready to use the next two minutes of the group's time. A timekeeper can be used. As in the 'go-round', no comments or questions should be allowed to follow the offerings.
- **Worship sharing**. This can be particularly suitable for potentially controversial, difficult or personal topics. It differs from creative listening, in that it is less based on thinking than on surrendering ourselves to worship and accepting what emerges. Although participants are asked to reflect on the questions in advance, contributions are likely to be at a deeper level, which may surprise the speakers themselves. Here, it usually is best to state the question or issue, and then start with a short period of silence (about 5 minutes) where each person moves into worship and thinks of the contribution they may feel called to make. People then speak in any order. Close with a period of silent worship.
- The emphasis is on worshipful listening.
- The group may agree before starting to place time limitations on each person so that everyone has a chance to speak. In this case, if one person is approaching the time limit, the facilitator should intervene to ask that the speaker come to a conclusion.
- An object may be used as a talking stick if the group would find it helpful.

Working in pairs or small groups of 3–4

Pairs or small groups give each person time to speak in depth. These reflections need not be reported back to the whole group.

- The listener should not speak, though non-verbal signs of attention are helpful.
- It is fine for the speaker to be silent for a while if they want.
- The listener should be reminded not to respond to the first speaker when it is their turn to speak.

Group Discussion

There may be times, especially in the activities for groups where the give-and-take of a discussion can be right, when a full flow of ideas is wanted, and this might encourage some Friends to venture making contributions they were cautious of offering in other modes. It will be particularly important to encourage the quiet or reticent and not to let one or two Friends dominate the group.

In discussion, the facilitator has three main aims.

- To enable all to participate, not just the articulate and long-winded.
- To keep the discussion to the point.
- To prevent heated feelings from turning the discussion into an argument.

It is quite appropriate to ask for a minute or two of silence at any point if the facilitator feels this will help the group. You can also suggest that the group moves into creative listening mode so the range of views can be heard without interruption.

Quick think (sometimes called a brainstorm)

Ideas are produced rapidly (but perhaps giving someone enough time to record them) without further discussion or questioning. This is useful for bringing up a lot of suggestions, which can then be used as material for a more reflective discussion.

Activities for personal reflection or for work with a spiritual friend: Listening to our life

The first activity is designed to enable you to investigate how far the text speaks to people – no matter how minimally this might be. The aim is to find the insights in the text which may be useful for us so that we might build on them, without being hampered by negative feelings of dislike or disagreement with the text. Then we wish to look at our lives. In so doing we can look again without the burden of guilt or fear, arrogance or complacency.

Activity 1a – Looking at the text
1. Consider the title of the text – Journey into Life – and think about why the author might have chosen this title.
2. What new light do I find in reading this text?
3. What aspects of the text are true to my experience?
4. What are the implications of this text for my life?
5. What problems do I have with the text?

Activity 1b – Probing the text
- Place the text on a scale of 0–10, depending on how much it spoke to you.

0 ————————————————————→10

Not at all   *Spoke to my condition completely*
- Wherever you placed yourself on the scale, make a list of those things which placed you at that point, not lower.
- Looking at your list, what strikes you as important or significant?
- Are there points where you would like to resonate more fully with aspects of the text?
- What prevents you?
- What is the smallest and easiest possible step you could take to enable this to happen?

Activity 2
For this activity you will need sheets of paper (A3 is best if people are drawing), and pens and pencils (a variety of colours is good).
   a) Looking over your whole life, draw/journal an overview of your

life, with the highs and lows of your life clearly marked and labelled.

This image could be in the form of:

- a line graph
- a route over a map
- a journey across key stepping stones
- any other visual image which demonstrates key events in your life
- at this stage, journaling could take the form of bullet points/ headlines/single sentences/one-word summaries.

b) Now redraw your image/revisit your brief summaries. This time use your image to show those points in your life where you were most truly guided by your Inner Clerk; where you acted most in concert with your deepest self; where you felt yourself to be most guided.

If you are journaling, use your writing to explore those points in your life you feel most drawn to. Try not to think too deeply – let your pen do the work and carry you lightly.

c) Looking at the two sets of images/sets of writing, make a list of those things which strike you and consider the following points:

- If you wished to deepen your journey, sense yourself living a life more deeply guided by your Inner Clerk, what things would you have to do? Make a list.
- What is the smallest and easiest possible step you could take?
- What prevents you from taking this?

Activities for small group reflection and discussion: Deepening our life in the spirit

These activities are most suitable for small groups (twos, threes or fours).

The story of a life given in the lecture offers a number of themes. With one or two others, spend some time noticing and sharing themes/ideas from the text. Use the following to prompt your reflection.

Journey
- early childhood
- impact of early childhood experiences
- early religious impulses and experiences.

Encounter
- encountering "a creative Energy that has birthed us and totally accepts us, unfolding an abundance of life for us, desiring we should be made whole" (see p. 7)
- the barriers which some of our early experiences, our history and culture might place in the way of this encounter
- finding evidence for the presence of this creative energy in the story of our own lives and experiences
- the Quaker story and the lives of the Early Friends providing metaphors for this encounter and its unfolding.

Transformation
- the potential in human life for transformation
- the cost of making love our first motion
- the necessity for a strong community in order to exemplify the outcomes of an encounter.

Questions for discussion
- Did any other themes strike you?
- Do any of the themes you have identified resonate with your life story?
- If you wished to deepen your journey, expand your experience of encounter, what help would you need from those around you?
- What help could you provide to others on their path?

Activities for larger group reflection and discussion: Building community where we are

These next activities consider how we might strengthen the community in which we find ourselves. These activities are most suitable for discussion in larger groups (anything from ten to twenty, or even your whole meeting).

For large groups or groups with people from more than one local meeting, you may decide to undertake some preliminary work in smaller groups (six or eight), with each group feeding back into a plenary session.

Reflect on the following discussions. You may want to record people's contributions in some way (for example on a flip chart).

For use by local or area meetings

For this activity you will need flip chart paper and pens.

The last paragraph of the text paints a picture of our Religious Society as a flourishing community:

> "a vibrant community where we bring our whole selves in order to be made whole; where we share with each other the difficult aspects of our journey, as well as the joys and the affirmations we find together; where our lives are made accountable to and for each other; in which we support and uphold each other as each of us strives towards that inner space where love can become our first motion; where each of us works to turn ourselves over to the Light, that power, which has the capacity to transform us." (see p. 39)

You are going to consider your local meeting or your area meeting in the light of this description. It doesn't matter where you think or feel your meeting is in relation to this quotation. The act of considering this together builds community. Remember to look at the situation with 'soft eyes'.

    a) Imagine your local meeting in five years' time. Imagine it has been transformed into your ideal local meeting.

- What would a visitor see, hear, notice, experience?

- What would be different for you?
- How would you be different?

b) On a scale of 0–10, working first on your own and then as a group, decide how accurate this is as a current description of, your local meeting or area meeting, Place it on the scale below.

0 $\longrightarrow$ 10

Not at all   *Describes my local meeting exactly*

- Wherever you placed your meeting on that scale make a list of those things which placed you at that point, not lower.
- Looking at your list, what strikes you as important or significant?
- What would make your local meeting a more nourishing place to worship?
- What is the smallest and easiest step to be taken in this direction?
- What do you need to do to enable this step to be taken?

Gerald Hewitson & Simon Best

Exploring further, digging deeper
Further reading

The following list is not meant to be either definitive or exhaustive, but a record of those books I have found helpful.

Finding our path, maintaining a practice

Ambler, Rex. *Light to Live by: An Exploration of Quaker Spirituality*. London: Quaker books, 2002.

Baldwin, Christina. *Life's Companion – Journal Writing as a Spiritual Practice*. New York: Bantam Books, 1991.

Brown, Elizabeth, and Alec Davison. *Journeying the Heartlands – exploring spiritual practices of Quaker worship*. United Kingdom: The Kindlers, 2009.

Hall, Thelma. *Too Deep for Words – Rediscovering Lectio Divina*. New York: Paulist Press, 1988.

Klassen, Joanne. *Tools for Transformation*. West Conshohocken: Infinity, 2004.

Laird, Martin. *Into the Silent Land: the practice of contemplation*. London: Darton, Longman and Todd, 2011.

Lampen, John, ed. *Seeing, Hearing, Knowing – Reflections on Experiment with Light*. York, England: William Sessions.

Progoff, Ira. *The Practice of Process Meditation: The Intensive Journal Way to Spiritual Experience*. New York: Dialogue House Library, 1980.

Smith, Cyprian. *The Way of Paradox – Spiritual Life as taught by Meister Eckhart*. London: Darton Longman and Todd, 2004.

Thich Nhat Hahn. *Peace in Every Step*. London: Bantam Books, 1991.

Wall, Ginny. *Deepening the Life of the Spirit: Resources for Spiritual Practice*. London: Quaker Books, 2012.

Other reflections

Chryssavgis, John. *In the Heart of the Desert*. Bloomington: Indiana World Wisdom, Inc. 2008.

Kelly, Thomas R. *A Testament of Devotion*. New York: Harper, 1992.

Kelly, Thomas R. *The Eternal Promise: A sequel to A Testament of Devotion*. New York: Second Friends United Press, 2006.

Punshon, John. *Encounter with Silence*. Richmond: Friends United Press, 1987.

Williams, Rowan. *Silence and Honey Cakes: The Wisdom of the Desert*. Oxford: Lion Hudson plc, 2004.

Woolman, John, ed. P Phillips. *The Journal and Major Essays*, Moulton. Richmond: Friends United Press, 2007.

Quaker background and history

Ambler, Rex. *Truth of the Heart: An Anthology of George Fox*. London: Quaker Books, 2007.

Baumann, Richard. *Let your words be few: Symbolism of speaking and silence among seventeenth century Quakers*. Cambridge: Cambridge University Press, 1983.

Dandelion, Ben Pink. *The Liturgies of Quakerism*. Aldershot: Ashgate Publishing Limited, 2005.

Gwyn, Douglas. *The Covenant Crucified: Quakers and the Rise of Capitalism*. London: Quaker Books, 2006.

Keiser, R. Melvin, and Rosemary Moore. *Knowing the Mystery of the Life Within: Selected Writings of Isaac Penington in their Historical and Theological Context*. London: Quaker Books, 2005.

Moore, Rosemary Anne. *The Light in their Consciences: the early Quakers in Britain 1646–1666*. Pennsylvania: State University Press, 2000.

Spencer, Carole Dale. *Holiness the Soul of Quakerism*. Milton Keynes: Paternoster, 2007.

Biblical and theological insights

Borg, Marcus J. *Jesus: Uncovering the life, teachings and relevance of a religious revolutionary*. New York: Harper Collins, 2008.

Borg, Marcus J. *Reading the Bible Again for the First Time*. New York: Harper Collins, 2002.

Boulton, David. *Who on Earth Was Jesus: The Modern Quest for the Jesus of History*. Winchester: O Books, 2008.

Myers, Ched. *Binding the Strong Man: a Political Reading of Mark's Story of Jesus*. New York: Orbis Books, 2008.

Wink, Walter. *Unmasking the Powers*. Philadelphia: Fortress Press, 1986.

Wink, Walter. *Engaging the Powers*. Minneapolis: Fortress Press, 1992.

Wink, Walter. *The Powers That Be*. New York: Doubleday, 1998.

General background and history

Hackett Fischer, David. *Albion's Seed: Four British Folkways in America*. New York: Oxford University Press, 1989.

Hill, Christopher. *The World Turned Upside Down – Radical Ideas During the English Revolution*. London: Penguin, 1991.

Hunt, Tristram. *The English Civil War at First Hand*. London: Orion Press, 2002.

Purkiss, Diane. *The English Civil War – A People's History*. London: Harper Perennial, 2007.

Stories and their function

Boyd, Brian. *On the Origin of Stories*. Cambridge, Mass: Harvard University, 2009.

Booker, Christopher. *The Seven Basic Plots: Why We Tell Stories*. London: Continuum, 2004.

Campell, Joseph. *The Hero with a Thousand Faces*. London: Fontana, 1993.

Endnotes

1   George Fox, edited by John Nickalls, *The Journal of George Fox* (Religious Society of Friends, 1952, rev. 1975), p. 27; *Quaker faith & practice (Qf&p)*, (Britain Yearly Meeting, 1995 and subsequent editions), §26.03. The 'flaming sword' is a reference to the Biblical story of Adam and Eve: an angel with a flaming sword is put to stand at the gates of Eden, preventing the return of Adam and Eve once they have been exiled (Genesis 3:24). George Fox offers the idea that we can return to Paradise here and now.

2   From a traditional Quaker phrase, 'To proceed as way opens'. This means "to wait for guidance, to avoid hasty judgment or action, to wait for future circumstances to help solve a problem. The spiritual guidance which may come in a time of seeking or entirely unexpectedly, bringing suggestion for previously unforeseen action." – Brent Bill, "Holy ordinary: Musings and photography from a Quaker perspective", http://holyordinary.blogspot.co.uk/.

3   Edward Burrough, "To the present distracted and broken nation" (1659); in *Qf&p* §23.11. There is no modern reprint of the Burrough pamphlet itself.

4   *Journeying the heartlands*, ed. Elizabeth Brown and Alec Davison (Kindlers, 2009), p. 1. The Kindlers are an experimental group based in North West London Area Meeting, working to rekindle the power of Quaker worship by renewing and deepening our spiritual practices.

5   Sandra Cronk: *Dark Night Journey* (Pendle Hill, 1991), p. 38. *"The Dark Night of the Soul"* was originally the title of a poem and treatise by St John of the Cross, written around 1580.

6   Fox, *Journal*, p. 14, and p. 21.

7 See Isaac Penington, ed. R. Melvin Keiser and Rosemary Moore, *Knowing the mystery of life within: Selected writings of Isaac Penington* (Quaker Books, 2005), especially Melvin Keiser's introduction to Part 2, pp. 121–22.

8 Fox, *Journal*, p. 32.

9 Fox, *Journal*, p. 168.

10 Penington, *Knowing the Mystery of Life Within*, p. 191.

11 From the manuscript "A history of the rise of Friends and progress of truth" not published in his lifetime; it can be found in Henry J. Cadbury, *Narrative papers of George Fox* (Friends United Press, 1972) p. 24, and in Hugh McGregor Ross, *George Fox speaks for himself* (Sessions, 1991) p. 73.

12 For example Amos 5:24; Luke 6:20–36. Gerard Guiton describes how the early Friends "were to be a community of reconciliation and healing, a Kingdom community striving for justice and mercy for all, including enemies but also for the materially poor, the powerless ones. Like Jesus, the Friends were prepared to suffer and die for that ineffable Love they believed was manifest in their individual and collective 'flesh and bone'. Only this Love and its liberating Kingdom – what may also be called the Rule, Covenant or Presence of Love, or Fox's term, the 'Covenant of Peace' – could heal the deep wounds of the single heart and that of the world." *The early Quakers and the Kingdom of God* (Inner Light Books, 2012), p. 3.

13 *Qf&p* §19.14.

14 Penington, *Knowing the mystery of life within*, p. 141; in *Qf&p* §26.70.

15 Kelly, *A Testament of Devotion*, p. 94.

16 *Qf&p* §19.07.

17 Fox, *Journal*, p. 56. The placing of the comma could make this seem ambiguously phrased to a modern reader: Fox is saying "they believed there was no such thing as anyone who could be free from sin".

18 See Walter Wink, *Unmasking the Powers* (Fortress Press, 1986), p. 27.

19 Epistle 16 (1652), in George Fox, *Works,* vol. 7, p. 24.

20 Penn, *No Cross, No Crown* ch.3, §1 (Sessions Book Trust, 1981), p. 30.

21 *Qf&p* §19.18.

22 Mark 1:23.

23 Letter from prison 'To all the dearly beloved people of God', around 1656; Nayler, *A collection of sundry books…* (1716).

24 *Qf&p* § 18.

25 "The world is, to a degree at least, the way we imagine it. When we think it to be godless and soulless, it becomes for us precisely that. And we ourselves are then made over into the image of godless and soulless selves. If we want to be made over into the image of God – to become what God created us to be – then we need to purge our souls of materialism and other worldviews that block us from realising the life God so eagerly wants us to have." Walter Wink, *The powers that be*, p. 14.

26 http://www.experiment-with-light.org.uk/ and Rex Ambler, *Light to live by* (Quaker Books, 2002).

27 Appleseed was developed by Brenda Clifft-Heales and the late Chris Cook. They gave the Swarthmore Lecture *Images and Silence* (Quaker Home Service, 1992), and published an Appleseed workbook *Seeding the spirit* (Woodbrooke, 2001).

28 Life Writing For Transformation was originated by Joanne Klassen, founder of Heartspace Writing School, and courses in it are held at Woodbrooke Quaker Study Centre.

29 *Qf&p* §19.33.

30 Pendle Hill, named after George Fox's hill of vision, is a Quaker study centre on the outskirts of Philadelphia: www.pendlehill.org.

31 *Qf&p* §19.08.

32 *Qf&p* §19.14.

33 *Qf&p* §19.12.

34 *Qf&p* §24.04.

35 Epistle 92 (1655).

36 Epistle 5, in *Works* (1831/1990), vol 7, p. 19.

37 *Advices & queries* 1. *Qf&p* §1.02.1.

38 Robert Putnam, in a lecture to Swarthmore College in the autumn of 2011, speaking on his book *American Grace: How Religion Divides and Unites Us* (Simon & Schuster, 2010).

39 *Qf&p* §19.32.

40 *Qf&p* §11.01.

41 *Qf&p* §19.21.

42 George Fox: Epistle 10, (1652); also in *Qf&p* §20.42.

43 Walter Wink, *Unmasking the Powers*, p. 1.

44 *A collection of sundry books...* (1716), p. 696; *Works*, vol. 4 (2009), p. 382.

45 See Ched Myers, *Binding the Strong Man*, p. 37.

46 "See how these Christians love each other" is how Tertullian is often quoted. He is describing how outsiders see the Christians. The full quote is: "'Look,' they say, 'how they love one another' (for they themselves hate one another); 'and how they are ready to die for each other' (for they themselves are readier to kill each other)." *Apologeticum* ch. 39, 7; Loeb edition. See also John 13:35.